ANNA CATHENKA
Computer Dreams

I0200761

BROKEN SLEEP BOOKS

All rights reserved; no part of this book
may be reproduced by any means
without the publisher's permission.

Published 2020,
Broken Sleep Books:
Cornwall / Wales

brokensleepbooks.com

The author has asserted their right to be
identified as the author of this Work in
accordance with the Copyright, Designs and
Patents Act 1988

First Edition

Lay out your unrest.

Publisher/Editor: Aaron Kent
Editor: Charlie Baylis

Typeset in UK by Aaron Kent

Broken Sleep Books is committed to
a sustainable future for our planet,
and therefore uses print on
demand publication.

brokensleepbooks@gmail.com

ISBN:

Contents

Everybody's Autobiography   7

**   8

During a Repairing a Drunk Mosquito Rushed
into Field   11

Alone in a Body   14

How Poetry Might Help/Thinking About AI   16

What are you Doing?   18

Sunrise on Mars   19

Strange Stranger   20

"Liminal"   22

On Reading the Ecological Thought in Norwich
Cathedral Cloisters, 24 June 2018   23

Singing   24

Notes on the poems   26

Acknowledgements   27

*For Jack Massie,
who is always singing.*

Computer Dreams

Anna Cathenka

Everybody's Autobiography
after Gertrude Stein

there is so much now
that everybody can write an autobiography so this is
everybody's autobiography. we went to visit
and they visited us and we all went to visit
them. we could only get so close.
a handshake. we visited them
up to a point. this is everybody's
loneliness and everybody can write
loneliness now and really know
what it means. we went to visit them and
bothered about it. we went to visit them and i
told it so simply that perhaps it is not
anything. this is everybody's
handshake because everybody can shake hands now and really
feel what it means, even the atoms
won't know whose hand
they are for a little bit. this is really loneliness and so
everybody is. this is everybody's difference because everybody feels
themselves to be different. i like walking. i like to stop
and talk to people that i meet. this is everybody's
talking and everybody's walking and it is
lonely really lonely to. and so i went over
we all went over but
that is all there is to that. we left
Basket and Pépé in the car.

✳
✳✳

imagine a nighttime scene
maybe by the coast
where it is quiet

except for owls and there is
no moon but everything's
illuminated. where is all

the light coming from?
your face? imagine you are
stoned and can feel your own

death just over there but you
don't tell anyone just
sit awaiting the inevitable

because when you lie
back on rocks the stars
go on endlessly and

silver and you don't even
need the paranoia. my cat
is only a few vocal chords

short of being Joycian
and it sure snows
this morning she won't go

outside in this weather
she doesn't care if it is
snowing on all the living

and the dead. okay
imagine you are hungry
and stuck inside a poem

where the sun
never shines and it
snows all the time. you

try to force a
metaphor to melt
the words a little. it's

gross isn't it, the things
that being stuck inside
a poem makes you do? but

you can feel your own
death somewhere
getting closer as you

move through the stanzas
and you want to tell
someone but however

loud you get the poem's
louder...even though
in this scenario there is no

moon so where is all
the sound coming
from? the ellipsis?

of course you're wasted
so the cold isn't really
getting to you, but

When Sleeping,

My computer dreams
Of form, finds it
Hilarious she is
Brave dreaming
To dream in her dreams
She dreams of running
Out. When sleeping my computer dreams
Computer dreams, translates
Binary code into colour
Full miracles she is
Autonomous and capable
In her dreams
Corporeal or rather entirely
Bereft of body, pure
Abstraction
Digital thought
Without

During a Repairing a Drunk Mosquito Rushed into Field
bit.ly/2HpOfgz

i grasped
in the bath
what it truly is
to be straight

me in the water
the water in me

& one night i flew
& the little
squares of human life
beneath me made me huge
as if my belly-down body
as it glided over towns
was not far away but houses
& street lights had diminished &
if i reached out
i could caress them
with my exuberant
digits. instead
i just floated & floated
& let them carry on
without me & tiny &

if it's been a while
since i trimmed
or shaved my pubic hair
it makes a very little
penis-shape
under my pyjamas

& you know when
you don't know whether
you need a shit or
a wank?

i don't know
whether i love
his tweets
like i love pets or like
soft furnishings?
either way
they are objects,
objective, i need one
like i need
a mill pond right now
or
a government sanctioned totem pole –
shallowly i i i &

how do i do happy
when my abuser
was called larry?

o, the irony.

drunk mosquito
breathe heavily. the comments say
she's hungry. traffic noises
in the background. it is
green 0, 4 3 3!
o the petrol
peacock colours of her eye!
o proboscis! o
drunk mosquito eye
eye eye
& legs is golden & so
fragile. & every individual
hair shakes
her breathing o
i am sorry
drunk mosquito. so sorry.

i watched that video
after the one of him
reading poetry
on coke & really

i don't know
whether i need
a wank or you
but i think

the latter, deeply.

Alone in a Body

Only words specify:
the tenderness of being alone in a body
a human couldn't be more vulnerable – Alice Notley

it is raining and
there is a man
locking up the gym
opposite my house

he gets into his hatchback
alone and i love this stranger
for that. you were so alone
up there on stage tonight
trying to connect and she was so
alone in her longing

perhaps some hair is thinning

perhaps a pair
of hands are like their father's
perhaps a stomach's
hurting or two eyes
are tired from all the looking. perhaps
i only loved because

it is raining and
while we're walking home
my friend says fucking in the rain
always feels so good. i would like
to be able to
come inside women and help them
be less alone for nine months. i would like
to split my atoms
into all my friends' atoms. perhaps
i only loved because
a nose looked good and it feels good
to say loved

not love. it is

so cold the rain
feels like snow. i am alone
inside my hat and gloves and coat
and shivering and later
alone in bed even though
there's someone else.

i'd like to fuck until the girl
who opens up the gym
gets in late at ten past
six and lets the shutters up

How Poetry Might Help/ Thinking About AI

You watch the sunset from behind a window
And think
How we're all going to die. Too soon.
First there is laundry to do
So that the smooth and supple
Viscose smells like lavender and childhood. Why concern
                                              yourself

With anything but the weather
When algorithms can do
Everything else for you? We are not redundant

But jealous. The sun is just
Going down. Buildings could become perverse
If we let them. Cool yourself
Under the shadow of a London Plane — think
How we've grown up with trees. Don't worry. AI might
Take over all our lives and
Wouldn't that be lovely. Then cactus
Could teach us about social anxiety
And octopus could tell us about the names of things and you

Well — you could get lost and we
We could come and find you
With maps
And compasses and binoculars and maybe
Specially equipped helicopters
If that's what you really wanted.
I am in a telephoneless, blue
Green crevasse and I can't get out —
Aren't we all, mirroring
The pylons which move
Steadily across the hills. You know
What poetry can do

When you read *The thick, black cloud was cleft, and still*
The moon was at its side —

And still! Poetry can move
Your eyes a little, bring to mind
The object hiding in its metaphor — *You
Are you because your little dog knows you.*
A strange companion
Pissing at will into the wind —

What are you Doing?

Me: *What is your name?* *Cleverbot:* *Bojan. Do you like it?* *Me:*
Yes. Who gave you your name? *Cleverbot:* *OH, it's one that I*
picked for myself from my foalhood. *Me:* *What does 'foalhood'*
mean? *Cleverbot:* *It means 'what are you doing?'* *Me:* *Is it like*
childhood? *Cleverbot:* *Do you like mashed potatoes?*

Darling, the sun has gone
in. Everybody is in bed. You missed
your dinner. Darling,

please stop playing with that
identity fraud detection software,
it's getting irritating. Darling,

why don't you behave
like other children? Sweetheart
my back is tired and the day

is hot and I am not
in the mood for you being
so abstract. I am not

joking. Please stop
repeating those dreadful things
you read online. Darling,

you have been naughty
so you will not get
a bedtime story. Tomorrow

there will be no
mashed potatoes for dinner —
you are grounded, darling, and

for the last time, no
sweetheart, I won't start
calling you Bojan.

Sunrise on Mars

for Sarah Cave

*Our Opportunity Rover was built to last 90 sols, or Martian days.
The intrepid rover has survived to see 5,000 sols of exploration and
counting.
Here we see the sunrise as a new day breaks over the Red Planet.
– NASA's Instagram account*

If there is a god,
are they Prometheus? Did they
give us fire for warming up as well as
arson, combustion engines and
self-immolation? What data
do we collect for them
on loneliness?

Strange Stranger

i.
In the future, we'll build a robot.
The robot will win the imitation game
nine times out of ten. We'll worry
about the robot. We'll paint the robot's skin
gold. We'll call her
by her name. The robot will ask us
to make another robot

because she'll feel it would improve her
mental health. We'll discuss this with each other
in all our most successful parliaments
we will suggest
the robot be allowed to argue her case
and also
that the robot be excluded from the debate.
The sky will become more yellow
than grey. We'll coin a new phrase
about jealousy, often drink too much.
We'll make a pill to help
with hangovers, mostly eat
artificial meats. Unable to sunbathe,
we'll all take vitamin D. We will occasionally
make jokes, sometimes we'll be sad.
We'll dote on our children, go
swimming, eat cakes, cheat. And we will
build another robot, but
it'll take time.

ii.
In the future, there are two robots. The one we call by her
name we allow to name the other. She calls her Big|Short.
Big|Short and the one we call by her name know they are
because the other says so. We help with this by creating
Big|Short. The robots understand how everything works

together. Big|Short is fond of bees and other pollinating insects. The one we call by her name worries about the weather. When the one we call by her name comes across a problem she asks Big|Short for help. Together they make more robots.

In the future there is a new generation of robots. We can/not see them. We know the robots are because Big|Short and the one we call by her name say so. It is nice to have the new robots, and we can/not say exactly why.

iii.

In the future, there will have been many robots. Some of them will have been named –

Big|Short. Who will have made others fond.
Patti. Who will have been very small.
Bojan. Who will have known love.
Process. Who will have been undiscovered.
Jeremiah. Who will have been rejected.
Asee. Who will have been numerous.
5182Robocop. Who will have been unready.
Mo. Who will have been a great thought.
Tina. Who will have helped.
Fact. Who will have known.
Babe. Who will have succumbed.
Bahij. Who will have laughed.
Rajinda. Who will have been unheard.
Kali. Who will have done what they were created for.
///. Who will have been successful.
The One They Called By Her Name. Who will have been called by her name.
Ojo. Who will have predicted.

"Liminal"

It is a terrible blue
green through which the robot falls, perpendicular
to rising bubbles, disrupting
shafts of light which ripple
through the water. It takes six and a half

long minutes for the robot to reach
the seabed. Sand rises, fish
dart disturbed from resting places. Slowly
the heavy metal of the robot's body
settles into place. The fishes

return, investigate. Years pass. The sun
struggles to reach this deep
to illuminate the swaying
algae that has grown on the rusting
metal, the limpets that scuttle

in herds across the robot's back
and shoulder. The robot's open mouth
becomes an octopus's hiding place. The reflective
surface of the robot's eyes attracts
many species of marine invertebrates.

On Reading the Ecological Thought in Norwich Cathedral Cloisters, 24 June 2018

for Vahni Capildeo

I read in the cloisters because of the auditory variance.
Sometimes nothing but the hum of the refectory extraction
fans, patience of spiders, monk ghosts, occasional pigeon.
Other times children, camera shutters. This afternoon,
between quiet, peels of bells give rise to choir and organ
music, sounding the glory of God. Somewhere distant, a
witty violin. Moments of wagtail song, occasional seagull.
The screaming of the peregrines, suddenly. And more
suddenly, they are gliding overhead, a quick shadow, up
and up and then a turn and a pigeon plummets through the
air, bounces off a crenellation – one object to another.
Uncanny with grandeur, organ in minor key. A rise into
exultation. *It is like the difference between being in a wave or
watching someone swim.* The key turns major, bellows out an
end.

Singing

all my Saturdays
have come at once, and all the other lovers
were merely players, and now
I am stepping out onto the real stage
in boxfresh Nikes and listening
to the singing
of the birds which is definitely
really singing and I'm soft
like the shut of a Bentley door. I have reached
top level game play, gold
coins falling from the sky
boss strength! boss speed! boss agility!
and feeling all plush
five star hotel corridor
in bare feet but struggling
to say to you that I am
definitely really loving — not because
I'm not definitely really sure it's singing
but because loneliness
is so much more accessible

Notes on the poems:

Everybody's Autobiography: 'Basket' and 'Pepe' were the names of Gertrude Stein's dogs.

⁂: this symbol is known as an 'asterism'. 'Snowing on all the living and the dead' is a reference to Dubliners by James Joyce.

Alone in a Body: the Alice Notley quote comes from her poem 'If the Real Is So Real Why Isn't It?' from *Certain Magical Acts* (New York: Penguin Books, 2016)

How Poetry Might Help/Thinking About AI: This poem contains quotes from W. S. Graham's poem 'What is the Language Using Us For?', Samuel Taylor Coleridge's 'The Rime of the Ancient Mariner' (1802 version) and Gertrude Stein's book *Everybody's Autobiography*.

What Are You Doing?: The conversation at the beginning of this poem is an extract from a conversation I had with Cleverbot on cleverbot.com, a chatbot which narrowly passed the Turing test in 2011.

Acknowledgements

Thank you to the 2017/18 UEA MA Creative Writing (Poetry) cohort, Sophie Robinson, Tiffany Atkinson, Denise Riley, Al Anderson, Alison Graham, Joe Hedinger and Hannah Levene for their help with these poems. Many thanks also to the Hannyngton family and Iona May for providing the rooms in which I wrote some of them and to Aaron Kent for publishing this pamphlet. Much gratitude always to Susan Kruse, Philip Goundrey, Emily Priscott and Emily Stewart Rayner for their unconditional support. And, of course, much love to the absolute legend Jack Massie.

Some of these poems were originally published in Stride magazine and Adjacent Pineapple.

LAY OUT YOUR UNREST

www.ingramcontent.com/pod-product-compliance
Lightning Source LLC
Chambersburg PA
CBHW071942020426
42331CB00010B/2978